WE ALL HAVE REASONS TO PRAISE GOD

LEARNING TO FIGHT THE GOOD FIGHT OF FAITH

Folake Hassan

The Righteous Publishing House

London UK

Copyright © Folake Hassan 2014

Unless otherwise stated all Scripture quotations are taken from The Amplified Bible (AMP)

All rights reserved. No part of this publication may be reproduced or transmitted in any form or by any means, electronic or mechanical, including photocopying, recording, or by any informative storage and retrieval system, without the written permission of the Author.

We All Have Reasons To Praise God

ISBN: 978-0-9928684-6-8

Published by The Righteous Publishing House

Flat 7, 93 Villiers Road

Willesden. London NW2 5QB

Visit Our Website at:

www.theblessedchristian.co.uk

Appreciation

I give all praises to God Almighty, who chose me and qualified me to be a carrier of His Anointing, a carrier of His Presence. I thank God for enduing me with His Wisdom. My sincere appreciation also goes to the men and women from every part of the world that God has used to minister His Words to bless me. I thank my children for their good attitudes that have enabled me to walk a good walk in my journey as a Christian. I thank my parents for nurturing and taking good care of me through my childhood and they still do today.

Table of Contents

Introduction 1

[1] ..... The Lord Forgives 11

[2] ..... The Lord Heals 17

[3] ..... The Lord Redeems 21

[4] ..... The Lord Beautifies 27

[5] ..... The Lord Satisfies Our Mouth with Goodness ... 29

[6] ..... The Lord Renew Our Youth 33

[7] ..... The Lord Executes Righteousness and Justice ... 35

[8] ..... The Lord Makes Known Unto Us His Ways 37

[9] ..... The Lord is a Merciful God 39

Becoming a Christian 43

Introduction

We all need to know how to lay hold of the Word of God and refuse to let go until it blesses us. It is necessary to know how to accept the good news the Word of God promises us and personalise them for our own use.

I love what the psalmist says in Psalm 46: 12-13 He says

> "Your vows are upon me, O God; I will
> render praise to You and give You
> thank offerings. For You have delivered
> my life from death, yes, and my feet
> from falling, that I may walk before
> God in the light of life and of the living"

We need say to ourselves every day, 'Lord, Your vows are upon me to give you thank offerings for You have delivered my life from death'. This should be our confession at all times. We should remember that God has delivered us from death. Some of us usually think that the only offering we can give to God is money, but our acts of gratitude, <u>worship and praise are also forms of offerings</u>. We must

<u>learn to give God praise diligently and effectively. Our Acts of Worship should always be unto the Lord and not a mere eye service offered to please men</u>. It must be between us and God, knowing that it is God we are actually serving.

God has done so much for all of us to enjoy in the land of the Living. God has done so much for our benefits; the best thing we can do for ourselves is to make the conscious efforts to learn how to honour God for all He has done for us and to accept His Blessings and to appropriate them through our acts of gratitude to God.

God did not owe us anything; Christ did not commit any crime that deserves death, but for our Salvation, He went to the cross. Therefore, we need not quarrel with God over the delay we may experience in the manifestation of some of God's blessings in our lives. Delays may be caused most of the times by our own ignorance or that of other people. Whoever we are and whatever we have is as a result of God's faithfulness, His acts of generosity and the promises and the covenant He made to bless us:

> **My covenant will I not break or profane, nor alter the thing that is gone out of My lips. (Psalm 89:34).**

<u>The Bible advices us to praise God for His mighty acts and to praise Him according to the abundance of his greatness; that everyone who has breath on them should always praise the Lord (Psalms 150: 2, 6)</u>

God's blessings upon our lives are not small; they are mighty according to Psalm 150:2

> ******Praise Him for His mighty acts; praise Him according to the abundance of His greatness! (Psalms 150:2)**

It is a shame that satan, sin and the systems of the world have twisted things so much to make humanity go through several unnecessary challenges, pain and sufferings that make them think that God is their number one enemy or that He is the one behind the troubles they have seen in their lives. The blessings of The Lord on Planet Earth is sufficient for all humanity to enjoy and have surplus leftover. Satan has placed so much training; efforts; systems and beliefs in places and in the minds of humanity that God is not good. But we thank God for disarming the plans of satan; making a public display of Gods victory over satan in our lives. We thank God for His good works and His Words that bear the testimonies of the faithfulness of our God; and His intentions and plan for us. I pray that everyone who reads this book will eventually agree to the truth that God loves them and that His purpose for each and every one of us is of good and not of evil.

<u>I believe that God's plans and purposes for each and every one of us is mighty; awesome and beautiful,</u> God's plans for us is not ugly, it is not full of trouble, it is not of a small, meagre, barely surviving plans that satan is trying to throw at us. Therefore, we should be glad and be ready to praise God at all times. The depths of God's love, His riches and wisdom no one can fathom (Job 11:7; Isaiah 40:28; Romans 11:33; Psalm 145:3)

We should not allow the challenges and the pains we go through in life to makes us to lose the blessings God has in store for us and which He has paid the price. We should be willing to fight the good fight of faith by dwelling and meditating on the Word of God, including putting up a good attitude in all situations.

All Christians and Church services should always allow the praise and worship of God to fill our minds, spirit, soul and body. To make all our services and our environments be a way of thanking God for all He has done for us and as a way of acknowledging His Lordship. We must express our sincere appreciation of the price God paid for us through our praise and our worship (See Psalm 100:4). We should always remember that God is a good God, and all His plans for us are of good and not of evil (Jeremiah 29: 11). We should always thank God for His Faithfulness. We should always thank God for all He did for us already, for what He is doing and for what He will do for us. We should always thank God for who He is.

We should make a list of how and when God has brought an improvement into our lives. How He has improved our living standard. How He meets our needs. How He brought a good transformation into our lives. His faithfulness to us in all areas. We may not have accomplished all our heart's good desires, but we are not where we used to be.

Calling to Remembrance:

***I could remember growing up without a good pair of shoes, but now I have almost lost count on the number of pairs of shoes God has given me the grace to sow to charity organisations in the past few years.

***I was raised in one room shared with other 4 sisters, whereas God gave me the grace to raise my children with each of them having their own rooms.

***Growing up, there were days my mum will have to pray to God to give her wisdom on how to get us dinner, but now, God has given me the grace to pay for someone's dinner regularly, and the list goes on and on.

Some of us need to think about how God has been good to us. How He has paid bills on our behalf and cancelled debt for our sake. So learn to praise God. Praising God should produce enough joy in us that makes us to be well at all times.

We should not allow anything or anyone to make us feel downcast at any time. We should always remember how God has been faithful to us; knowing He will never leave us nor forsake us in The Name of Jesus Christ.

We should never allow anyone or any situation to makes us think that God is not good. We should never allow any being or any spirit to makes deposits into our lives that will makes us walk in sorrow, pain, sadness or shame. We should never allow ourselves to be the object of pity parties as well. No one should have enough authority to make us feel downcast at any time. We should always look at the bright side of life, looking to God through His Words, knowing that whatever challenges we may be going through are only temporary, knowing that there is a time for everything in life and that our joy and victories shall soon manifest itself for all eyes to see in The Name of Jesus Christ.

Have you ever wondered whether it is necessary to praise God at all despite all you have been through or are going through? I have good news for you. Yes, it is necessary to develop a good heart of gratitude towards God while we are waiting for the manifestation of His promises. Christ will not go to the cross a second time for us, He has already. Christ was nailed to the cross for our sins and He carried the penalties we are supposed to carry such that we do not have to bear our pains ourselves (Isaiah 53: 4-5). All we have to do is to study God's Word to know how we can receive our inheritance in Christ. We must not allow anyone or anything or any system to make us think that God is not good. We should learn to fight the good fight of faith by learning to study and stay on the Word of God until we see the manifestations of God's glory and the good plans He has for our lives. While we are waiting for our blessings to manifest, we may encounter some challenges along the journey of life which may be in other to mould and develop our characters <u>so that when the blessings come, we will be mature to handle them and not allow the blessings, the riches or arrogance and pride to destroy us (God forbid).</u>

Challenges do not mean that God is not good. If our attitudes towards God are right, then our attitudes towards men will be good and that will quicken the release of God's blessings to us.

<u>We should always go through the Scriptures and find out what God is saying concerning us and the situations we are facing</u> and especially the truth that God has already provided for our needs. He wants us to be blessed and then become a blessing to our generations. If we cannot see the manifestations of the blessings yet, then we should pray fervently to God asking Him to reveal to us what could be hindering our prayers.

**My prayer is that as you go through this book, you will find healing and deliverance and be made free from all forms of satanic bondages. I pray that you will have reasons to always give thanks and praise God in The Name of Jesus Christ.

The Bible advices us that we should always give praises unto the Lord. Looking away from all that satan and its kingdom, the systems of this world, the opinion of men, ignorance and traditions is trying to make us to (Hebrew 12:2).

In the book of 1 Thessalonians 5:17 the Bible advices us to thank God in all things no matter what the circumstances may be. This does not mean that we should be celebrating or dancing when we should be sober. But if satan is trying to push us into despair while others are rejoicing, then we have the right to disagree with such evil spirit. We have the right to refuse what satan is planning to give to us at all cost; we have the right not to accept what satan is trying to dish out for us. It will be of a great blessing for each and every one of us if we walk and agree with the Word of God concerning His purposes for our lives, for His purposes are good and not of evil (Jeremiah 29:11). There must have been good reasons for God to have said we should give Him thanks in all things. God must know something we have not yet discovered. Looking at our individual lives one way or the other, or looking around us, we should have reasons to praise God. There is a saying that "everyone that knows how to think will know how to thank God" therefore be more thankful.

***The fact that the mansions we desired have not manifested yet does not mean that God will not bring it to pass.

***For those trusting God for healing and health, my advice is that you should pay more attention to God by listening to what He will tell you through His

Words and then obey. God's instructions are not burdensome; His yoke is easy to bear.

We all have millions of reasons to always praise God. He saves our lives from destructions. He supplies all our needs.

For example: each time there is a rain, we should always remember to thank God. No one can shower the earth the way God does, no one has the capacity of watering the whole of the earth the way God does. With rain our crops grow; we have water to use for several purposes; rain cleans the air and the atmosphere thereby making the earth planet breathable and habitable.

Apart from what we can see physically, the Bible is full of the power of God and the reasons to always praise Him. Do not allow anything or anyone to paint the wrong picture in your mind that God is not good. Job in the Bible refused to curse God when he was even advised to do so (Job 2:9). Job's good attitude was what qualified him eventually to receive double blessings for all he lost (Job 42: 8-10).

I love the way the Psalmist, David speaks to his own soul and commands it to bless the Lord as in the Book of Psalm 103. I pray that this book will remind each and every one of us of what God has done for us; and instead of asking God to bless us all the time, we can then say to our soul to bless the Lord by praising God.

The Scriptures reference for this book is: Psalm 103

[1].....The Lord Forgives

"Who forgives [every one of] all your iniquities" (Psalm 103:3a)

Every one means all, all of our iniquities. The Lord specialises in forgiving and nullifying sins. You may be saying, oh I am a very righteous person. What I would say on that is, we are all righteous because of the Blood shed by our Lord and Saviour on our behalf. Therefore, our righteousness is of Him. Christ is the one who makes us righteous (Isaiah 54:17).

Psalmist David wrote: "in sin did my mother conceive me" (Psalm 51:5) we are all born into a sinful world but we thank God who made us to become righteous through Christ.

> "Giving thanks to the Father, Who has qualified and made us fit to share the portion which is the inheritance of the saints (God's holy people) in the Light. (Colossians 1.12)"

According to this verse of the Bible you can see that **forgiveness is our inheritance** as the children of the Most High God.

Giving thanks to the Lord in Whom we have our redemption through His blood, (which means) the **forgiveness** of our sins. (Colossians 1:14)

Also, as a true child of God, there is no condemnations for us, for the law of the Spirit of life in Christ Jesus has made us free from the law of sin and death. (Romans 8: 1-2)

> "THEREFORE, [there is] now no condemnation (<u>no adjudging guilty of wrong) for those who are in Christ Jesus,</u> who live [and] walk not after the dictates of the flesh, but after the dictates of the Spirit. For the law of the Spirit of life [which is] in Christ Jesus [the law of our new being] has freed me from the law of sin and of death"
> (Romans 8:1-2)

Do not dwell on the challenges you are going through. The Bible advices that we should cast down every imagination that exalts itself above the knowledge of Christ (2 Corinthians 10:5). The only things we should fix our minds on is The Word of God (Joshua 1:8; Isaiah 26:3)

Challenges are meant to train, develop, and prepare us for our God's given assignment. They are meant to shape us and make us to become wise in how we handle things.

As for the sufferings and pains that situations is putting on our ways, the Bible advices us to look away from them, meaning do not pay too much attention to them. They are just the distractions the enemy is trying to use to stop us from acknowledging the goodness of God in our lives. But I can assure the readers of this book and all my friends around the world that concerning us, satan failed the day Jesus paid the price for our redemption with His own blood; satan lost the day Jesus rose from death.

"THEREFORE THEN, since we are surrounded by so great a cloud of witnesses [who have borne testimony to the Truth], let us strip off and throw aside every encumbrance (unnecessary weight) and that sin which so readily (deftly and cleverly) clings to and entangles us, and <u>let us run with patient endurance and steady and active persistence</u> the appointed course of the race that is set before us, Looking away [from all that will distract] to Jesus, Who is the Leader and the Source of our faith [giving the first incentive for our belief] and is also its Finisher [bringing it to maturity and perfection]. He, for the joy [of obtaining the prize] that was set before Him, endured the cross, despising and <u>ignoring the shame</u>, and is now seated at the right hand of the throne of God" (Hebrews 12:1-2)

The challenges, pain, sickness and troubles we go through are distractions and the weapons that satan is trying to use to set enmities between us and our God. You can render satan's tools, power and strategies useless by allowing the Word of God to dwell in you richly.

Scriptures That Asures Us That God Forgives Sins

Blessed (happy, fortunate, to be envied) is he who has forgiveness of his transgression continually exercised upon him, whose sin is covered (Psalm 32:1)

For this is My blood of
the new covenant, which [ratifies the
agreement and] is being poured out for
many for the forgiveness of sins
(Matthew 26:28)

God exalted Him to His right hand to be
Prince and Leader and
Saviour and Deliverer and Preserver,
in order to grant repentance to Israel
and to bestow forgiveness and release
from sins (Acts 5:31)

To Him all the prophets testify (bear
witness) that everyone who believes in
Him [who adheres to, trusts in, and
relies on Him, giving himself up to Him]
receives forgiveness of sins through His
Name (Acts 10:43)

[2].....The Lord Heals

"Who heals [each one of] all your diseases" (Psalms 103:3b)

You do not have to carry the sickness in your body anymore. The Bible declares that the Lord healed all and each one of our diseases. You do not give any sickness the right to reside on your body; you do not tolerate sickness. You have the authority to agree with the Word of God and not with sickness. Whatever we allow on earth is what is allowed.

What Christ paid for is our wellbeing and not our sickness. No parent will pay for sickness to dwell on their children or to be delivered to their children. Most parents will pay for healing and good health to be delivered to their children and so is our heavenly Father God.

Total healing and good health is the plan of God for all humanity right from the creation which was the reason why God put in place all our needs right before creating us.

The adage "Health is wealth" is a true statement. The Lord God has no delight in sickness, people being sick does not pleasure God.

We should all work hard, pray regularly, and seek to be in good health always in spirit, soul and body. It is important to always remember that what we have is good health and not sickness.

All of us have several reasons to praise God continually. He heals all of our sicknesses, from minor sickness to a major sickness. He did not allow the calamities of this world to overcome or wipe us away. Above all, the Lord has delivered us from all evils by carrying the chastisements for us to obtain peace in His own body.

Healing Scriptures From The Bible

"But He was wounded for our transgressions, He was bruised for our guilt and iniquities; the chastisement [needful to obtain] peace and well-being for us was upon Him, and with the stripes [that wounded] Him we are healed and made whole" (Isaiah 53:5)

"He went once for all into the [Holy of] Holies [of heaven], not by virtue of the blood of goats and calves [by which to make reconciliation between God and man], but His own blood, having found and secured a complete redemption (an everlasting release for us)" (Hebrews 9:12)

He sends forth His word and heals them and rescues them from the
pit and destruction (Psalm 107:20)

[3].....The Lord Redeems

"Who redeems your life from the pit and corruption" (Psalm 103:4a)

It is a joy to discover and know that the Lord has saved us from going into the pit of hell. We can never go to the pit because we have been redeemed from going thereby virtue of the price paid by Christ. The pit of hell is not our destination and nothing should be big enough to push us to the place where we do not belong. Our Lord and Saviour has already stopped such evil from happening to us. He will not allow errors, mistakes, wrong desires, wrong motives, greediness and theft to have power over us.

Corruption will not be our portion, for the Lord will give His angels charge over us. The Lord God will give us The Holy contentment to be satisfied with what He has provided for us and not to be covetous of other people's gifts.

Prayer: I pray now that our eyes of understanding will be enlightened for us to see that no matter where God places us, we are surrounded by God's abundance and blessings. We have what we need; therefore corruption will not have dominion over us in The Name of Jesus Christ.

The Lord will not allow wrong desires to destroy any one of us in the Name of Jesus Christ.

Prayer: For those who have wondered away from their blessings, the Lord in His infinite mercy will restore each and every one of us back to His original purposes and blessings where we will all eat our bread without scarcity and without sorrow in The Name of Jesus Christ. The Lord will restore us back to His Place of blessing where poverty will not have access in The Name of Jesus Christ.

> For I know the thoughts and plans that
> I have for you, says the Lord, thoughts
> and plans for welfare and peace and
> not for evil, to give you hope in your
> final outcome. (Jeremiah 29:11)

There is no Death in Christ

If you are a Christian, I mean a born again child of God, you have to be clear about what the Lord did for you the day you accepted Christ as your Lord and Saviour; it was that you passed from death to life, therefore we say, there is no death in Christ.

"I assure you, most solemnly I tell you, the person whose ears are open to My words [who listens to My message] and believes and trusts in and clings to and relies on Him Who sent Me has (possesses now) eternal life. And he does not come into judgment [does not incur sentence of judgment, will not come under condemnation], but he has already passed over out of death into life. Believe Me when I assure you, most solemnly I tell you, the time is coming and is here now when the dead shall hear the voice of the Son of God and those who hear it shall live" (John 5: 24-25).

Because he has set his love upon Me, therefore will I deliver him; I will set him on high, because he knows and understands My name [has a personal knowledge of My mercy, love, and kindness—trusts and relies on Me, knowing I will never forsake him, no, never]. He shall call upon Me, and I will answer him; I will be with him in trouble, I will deliver him and honour him. With long life will I satisfy him and show him My salvation. (Psalm 91:14-16)

But be glad and rejoice forever in that which I create; for behold, I create Jerusalem to be a rejoicing and her people a joy. And I will rejoice in Jerusalem and be glad in My people; and the sound of weeping will no more be heard in it, nor the cry of distress. There shall no more be in it an infant who lives but a few days, or an old man who dies prematurely; for the child shall die a hundred years old, and the sinner who dies when only a hundred years old shall be [thought only a child, cut off because he is] accursed. They shall build houses and inhabit them, and they shall plant vineyards and eat the fruit of them. They shall not build and another inhabit; they shall not plant and another eat [the fruit]. For as the days of a tree, so shall be the days of My people, and My chosen and elect shall long make use of and enjoy the work of their hands. They shall not labor in vain or bring forth [children] for sudden terror or calamity; for they shall be the descendants of the blessed of the Lord, and their offspring with them. And it shall be that before they call I will answer; and while they are yet speaking I will hear.

Then the Lord said, My Spirit shall not forever dwell and strive with man, for he also is flesh; but his days shall yet be 120 years. (Genesis 6:3)

But if you are guided (led) by the [Holy] Spirit, you are not subject to the Law. (Galatians 5:18)

See also: Galatians 5:19-26

[4].....The Lord Beautifies

> "Who beautifies, dignifies, and crowns you with loving-kindness and tender mercy" (Psalm 103:4b)

The Lord is the only one that makes us beautiful. If you have ever wondered whether you are beautiful or not, or you desire to be more beautiful. I can assure you that in Christ you are beautiful, and in Christ, you can be more beautiful. Everyone and everything God made are beautiful:

> And God saw everything that He had made, and behold, it was very good (suitable, pleasant) and He approved it completely......... (Genesis 1:31)

If you have lost a bit of your beauty or you desire to be more beautiful, I will advise you to digest the word of God daily by studying the Holy Bible and allowing the Word of God to purge you of all dead works, worries, anxieties and unrighteousness. The Bible recorded that it is in His presence we have our fullness of joy: (Psalm 16: 10-11)

> For You will not abandon me to Sheol (the place of the dead), neither will You

> suffer Your holy one [Holy One] to see corruption. You will show me the path of life; in Your presence is fullness of joy, at Your right hand there are pleasures forevermore (Psalm 16: 10-11).

We are all beautiful in the sight of God, and if there is any part of our body or behaviour that needs improvements or refinement, at the appropriate time the Lord will glorify Himself by perfecting that which concerns us in The Name of Jesus Christ. The Bible says The Lord made everything beautiful in its time (Ecclesiastes 3:11). The Lord will give to us the ability to keep our body holy and beautiful for Him in The Name of Jesus Christ.

> Do you not know that your body is the temple (the very sanctuary) of the Holy Spirit Who lives within you, Whom you have received [as a Gift] from God? (1 Corinthians 6:19)

Anytime I think of worrying about my look or the thought of aging, God always put me in remembrance of His promises (Psalm 103:4b) that He is The One who beautifies me, even the thought and the assurance from the Word of God always calm down my worries and refreshes my spirit. I thank God for His Word.

[5].....The Lord Satisfies Our Mouth with Goodness

"Who satisfies your mouth [your necessity and desire at your personal age and situation] with good" (Psalm 103:5a)

Prayer: Father God, give us good stories to tell, empower us to say the right thing always.

What we should confess is the Word of God, not our feelings, not what a circumstance is dictating to us.

The Bible advices that The Word of God must not depart from our mouth, we must wright and right good scriptures down and read them to ourselves daily.

> **This Book of the Law shall not depart out of your mouth, but you shall meditate on it day and night, that you may observe and do according to all that is written in it. For then you shall make your way prosperous, and then**

**you shall deal wisely and have good
success. (Joshua 1:8)**

Walking with God, studying and obeying His Word helps to sanctify our speech. When we constantly study the Word of God and have it dwell in us richly, it will shape what we say, and our words will align with the Word of God. Developing the habit of studying the Word of God regularly can help us not to confess the wrong negative words that satan and situations intends for us to say.

Though it may take a while before we can completely adjust to this system of confessing the Word of God, but eventually it will become our habit to release through our mouth the words of life, words that are wholesome and full of grace. It takes practise and it may take time, but I can assure you that as we all continue studying and dwelling on the Word of God, what we say will eventually bless us in The Name of Jesus Christ.

There have been a few time when I wanted to be worrying about the foods I eat in the natural, and I remembered that it is God who sanctify whatever I put in my mouth holy, believing that He will not allow me to eat any contaminating food.

Also, we must have the believe that The Lord will sanctify our speech to bless us and to bring glory and honour to His Name, He will not allow any corrupt communication to flow through us in The Name of Jesus Christ

[6].....The Lord Renew Our Youth

".....so that your youth, renewed, is like the eagle's [strong, overcoming, soaring]!" (Psalm 103:5b)

The advantage which the Word of God gives us if we continue to study and obey it, is that it will purge us of all evil reports that may be flowing around thereby making us to be well. It will renew us much better than that of the eagles. The Bible admonishes us to renew ourselves and our minds by constantly studying The Word of God.

By constantly studying the Word of God, we will be free from all forms of worries.

> **Do not be conformed to this world (this age), [fashioned after and adapted to its external, superficial customs], but be transformed (changed) by the [entire] renewal of your mind [by its new ideals and its new attitude], so that you may prove [for yourselves] what is the good and acceptable and**

perfect will of God, even the thing which is good and acceptable and perfect [in His sight for you]. (Romans 12:2)

[7].....The Lord Executes Righteousness and Justice

> "The Lord executes righteousness and justice [not for me only, but] for all who are oppressed"
> (Psalm 103:6)

Righteousness and justice are important benefits that God can execute on behalf of all Christians that do His will. For those praying and asking God for justice, as you continue to attend to the Word of God through studies and prayers, the results we will see around us will be great; awesome and pleasant. Even some results that we think are not necessary or not good may actually be from God as part of His plans to help us develop in faith. He said "how many of you will give stones instead of bread to his children. The Lord will always give us the answer that will be of benefit to us; though it may not meet our immediate gratifications, but eventually we will have reasons to praise God.

The children of God did not find their journey from Egypt to The Promised Land interesting, hence they complained; yet it was the plan of God to take them to the Promised Land. I am sure some of us have been through some unpleasant experiences in life that seems as if it will not go away, but later to see that the result of all the trials is for our own good. There was a particular year when all the appliances in my flat packed up, because they all need to be replaced. Most of them as at then had been in use for over 15 years and at about the same time, my landlord launched a major refurbishment of my flat. While the work was going on, it looked as if the hell had broken loose on me; but seeing the result of the work and the grace that God gave me and my children to replace all the appliances, I can say that our endurance produced a good result.

> **But no weapon that is formed against you shall prosper, and every tongue that shall rise against you in judgment you shall show to be in the wrong. This [peace, righteousness, security, triumph over opposition] is the heritage of the servants of the Lord [those in whom the ideal Servant of the Lord is reproduced]; this is the righteousness or the vindication which they obtain from Me [this is that which I impart to them as their justification], says the Lord. (Isaiah 54:17)**

[8].....The Lord Makes Known Unto Us His Ways

> "He made known His ways [of righteousness and justice] to Moses, His acts to the children of Israel" (Psalm 103:7)

Only genuine friends will reveal to you their plans; most friends will wants to hide their plans from their friends so that they will be the only one that receives the accolade.

One of the reasons to always praise God is that He will always make known to us His ways and His Acts. He will always show us His next action concerning our lives. He will not leave us in the darkness of this world nor leave us in ignorance. He will always reveal to us His plans, the right things to do and He will reveal to us His will for our lives. This even becomes more effective as we continue to walk more with Him. We will be able to hear God clearly as we give Him more of our time.

> I do not call you servants (slaves) any longer, for the servant does not know what his master is doing (working out).

But I have called you My friends, because I have made known to you everything that I have heard from My Father. [I have revealed to you everything that I have learned from Him.] (John 15:15)

I love those who love me, and those who seek me early and <u>diligently</u> shall find me. (Proverbs 8:17)

Constantly walking with God enables us to discover the mind of God.

[9].....The Lord is a Merciful God

> "The Lord is merciful and gracious,
> slow to anger and plenteous in
> mercy and loving-kindness" (Psalm
> 103: 8)

The Lord God is full of mercy, <u>He has not dealt with us according to our sins</u> neither has he rewarded us according to our iniquities. Several places in the Bible, the Lord God shows mercy to people we thought were undeserving of the Blessings of The Lord. Example was Apostle Paul before his conversion, he witnessed that he was the worst sinners of all.

> **The saying is sure and true and worthy**
> **of full and universal acceptance, that**
> **Christ Jesus (the Messiah) came into**
> **the world to save sinners, of whom I am**
> **foremost. (1Timothy 1:15)**

Despite all, the Father God forgave Him and even anointed him to do mighty wonders.

If you have been thinking that maybe you do not qualify for God's Best, I would want you to have a change of attitude from today; God's plan for His children and His chosen ones is of good and not of evil. Always have it at the back of your mind that it is possible for God to bless you.

Your past is not your future. As you continue to attend to the Word of God; as you continue to listen to Him and obey His instructions, as you continue to pray regularly to God; as you continue to serve Him, I can assure you that what you will receive from God will always be the best.

The Bible emphasises that God shows mercy and loving-kindness toward those who reverently and worshipfully fear Him (Psalm 103:11). No one can fear the God they do not know. Hence the reason for us to study The Bible always. To start developing the honour and the respect due to God, we need to develop a relationship with Him by being close to Him through His Word, by having regular fellowship with Him, constantly doing this will refine us and make us to be created in God's image.

As soon as we start developing the attitude of honouring and referencing God, His blessings will come upon us automatically. Discovering the mind of God will enable us to enjoy the blessings of God without interruption. But it requires a bit of effort from our own side which is just simply to study The Holy Bible and obey its instructions. (See Psalm 103:17-20)

***I pray that the Lord God will raise more Pastors and Evangelist for us that will proclaim the truth of God's Words from generation to generation in The Name of Jesus Christ.

Becoming a Christian

Becoming a Christian is not a difficult task at all. The Holy Bible instructs every mankind to be born again by confessing our sin and accept Jesus Christ as our Lord and Saviour by praying a simple prayer of salvation.

Prayer of Salvation

Father God, I come to You in the Name of Jesus Christ. According to your Word in the book of Roman 10:9, which says "If you acknowledge and confess with your lips that Jesus is Lord and in your heart believe (adhere to, trusts in, and rely on the truth) that God raised Him from the dead, you will be saved.
I confess Jesus Christ as my Lord and Saviour, Lord Jesus come into my life and forgive me for all my sins. Be Lord of my life in Jesus name, Amen.

Congratulations if you have just prayed this prayer, you are now a Christian and you are saved.

You now have rights to all the promises of God in the Holy Bible.

I will advise you to read the Holy Bible and other Christian literatures regularly to build up your faith in the Lord. Also you will need a Word based church to attend regularly i.e. be part of a good local church that teaches Christian to grow in The Word of God.

*****Please write to us through our website contact page at www.theblessedchristian.co.uk to inform us of your new decision you made to become a Christian and we will continue to offer all helps necessary for you to grow in Christ.

Remain Blessed

Yours in Christ

Folake Hassan (Mrs)

Founder/President: The Blessed Christian Centre

About The Author

Folake Hassan is the Owner of The Online Christian Bookshop named The Blessed Christian: www.theblessedchristian.co.uk . She is the Author of the books titled "The Attributes of God" and "Coming Out of Bondage" and "We All Have Reasons to Praise God". It is Folake's passion to see souls saved and confess Jesus Christ as their Lord and Saviour. Folake Hassan is blessed with 3 children with the youngest being 18 years of age at the time of writing this book. Folake and her children live in London, United Kingdom.

About The Book

As The Children of The Almighty God, no situation should make us feel sorry for ourselves. If what you are trusting God for is delayed, that does not mean that God will not come true for you too. Learn to rejoice and give God the thanks in the midst of your waiting knowing that trusting God has a good reward.

www.ingramcontent.com/pod-product-compliance
Lightning Source LLC
Chambersburg PA
CBHW020023050426
42450CB00005B/615